· THE ·
FIVE
HAZARDOUS
ATTITUDES

STUDY GUIDE

Cover design by Sara Young
Author photo on cover by Andrew van Tilborgh

ISBN: 978-1-960678-87-4   1 2 3 4 5 6 7 8 9 10

Printed in the United States of America

STUDY GUIDE

· THE ·
FIVE
HAZARDOUS
ATTITUDES

1. Anti-authority
2. Invulnerability
3. Macho
4. Impulsivity
5. Resignation

Ways to Win the War Within

RICKY BROWN

A V A I L

CONTENTS

THE
FIVE
HAZARDOUS
ATTITUDES

1. Anti-authority
2. Invulnerability
3. Macho
4. Impulsivity
5. Resignation

Ways to Win the War Within

RICKY BROWN

DON'T TELL ME: ANTI-AUTHORITY

Plainly put, Anti-Authority is the Hazardous Attitude found in people who don't like anyone telling them what to do.

READING TIME

As you read
Chapter 1:
"Don't Tell
Me: Anti-
Authority"
in *The Five
Hazardous
Attitudes*,
reflect on,
and respond
to the text by
answering
the following
questions.

REFLECT AND TAKE ACTION:

What is "Anti-Authority"? How would you define it in your own words?

_____

_____

_____

_____

_____

_____

_____

_____

_____

_____

What are some reasons people may develop an Anti-Authority attitude?

_____

_____

_____

_____

_____

_____

_____

_____

_____

_____

How can unresolved trauma contribute to the development of Hazardous Attitudes?

_____

_____

_____

_____

_____

_____

_____

_____

Why may higher compensation not necessarily change a person's Anti-Authority attitude?

_____

_____

_____

_____

_____

_____

_____

_____

What impact does a Hazardous Attitude of Anti-Authority have on a person's relationships and reputation in the community?

_____

_____

_____

_____

_____

_____

_____

_____

How did the actions of authority figures in Tony's life contribute to forming his Hazardous Attitude?

_____

_____

_____

_____

_____

_____

_____

_____

_____

Explain why people with a Hazardous Attitude believe there is a sufficient reason to break rules. Have you ever done this?

_____

_____

_____

_____

_____

_____

_____

_____

What role does self-awareness play in changing a person's Hazardous Attitude?

_____

_____

_____

_____

_____

_____

_____

_____

Describe the consequences of placing someone with an Anti-Authority attitude in a role that requires repetitive rule-following.

_____

_____

_____

_____

_____

_____

_____

_____

_____

Define the compounding nature of Hazardous Attitudes. What are the potential outcomes?

_____

_____

_____

_____

_____

_____

_____

_____

_____

IT WON'T HAPPEN TO ME: INVULNERABILITY

Invulnerability is the attitude that causes people to believe that consequences happen to others but not to them.

READING TIME

As you read Chapter 2: "It Won't Happen to Me: Invulnerability" in *The Five Hazardous Attitudes*, reflect on, and respond to the text by answering the following questions.

REFLECT AND TAKE ACTION:

What is the Hazardous Attitude of Invulnerability? How would you define it in your own words?

_____

_____

_____

_____

_____

_____

_____

_____

_____

How does the nursery rhyme about Jack jumping over a candlestick relate to the concept of Invulnerability?

_____

_____

_____

_____

_____

_____

_____

_____

_____

_____

Give an example from this chapter that illustrates how people often act with an Attitude of Invulnerability in various aspects of their lives.

_____

_____

_____

_____

_____

_____

_____

_____

Explain the immediate consequences that individuals may face due to the Hazardous Attitude of Invulnerability.

_____

_____

_____

_____

_____

_____

_____

_____

Discuss the common theme of entrepreneurs facing skepticism from friends and family. How does this relate to the Hazardous Attitude of Invulnerability?

_____

_____

_____

_____

_____

_____

_____

_____

_____

_____

Describe how the "can't help it" mindset contributes to the Hazardous Attitude of Invulnerability.

_____

_____

_____

_____

_____

_____

_____

_____

_____

_____

Analyze the negative impact of skill and luck when they become "terrible roommates," particularly for someone with an Attitude of Invulnerability.

_____

_____

_____

_____

_____

_____

_____

_____

_____

Explore the consequences of willful ignorance and how it affects people with an Attitude of Invulnerability.

_____

_____

_____

_____

_____

_____

_____

_____

_____

Explain how the insatiable appetite for more, as highlighted in this chapter, intensifies the Hazardous Attitude of Invulnerability.

_____

_____

_____

_____

_____

_____

_____

_____

_____

CHAPTER 3

MACHO: I CAN DO IT

*Macho is an attitude that is found
in people who constantly feel the
need to prove themselves.*

READING TIME

As you read
Chapter 3:
"Macho: I
CAN DO IT"
in *The Five
Hazardous
Attitudes*,
reflect on,
and respond
to the text by
answering
the following
questions.

REFLECT AND TAKE ACTION:

Define the Hazardous Attitude of Macho.
How would you describe this attitude in
your own words?

_____

_____

_____

_____

_____

_____

Discuss the mantra of individuals with
a Macho attitude, as mentioned in this
chapter.

_____

_____

_____

_____

_____

Analyze the relationship between the
over-inflated sense of self-ability and the
willingness to take risks.

_____

_____

_____

_____

_____

Describe the consequences of a person with a Macho attitude trying to overcompensate for events they cannot control.

_____

_____

_____

_____

_____

_____

_____

_____

_____

Examine the consequences of the "I can do it" mentality and its connection to the Hazardous Attitude of Macho.

_____

_____

_____

_____

_____

_____

_____

_____

_____

Explore the significance of letting go and avoiding unnecessary confrontations, especially in professional settings.

_____

_____

_____

_____

_____

_____

_____

_____

_____

Discuss the metaphor of holding onto offense and unforgiveness as drinking poison and hoping someone else will die and how it relates to the Hazardous Attitude of Macho.

_____

_____

_____

_____

_____

_____

_____

_____

_____

IMPULSIVITY: DO SOMETHING!

Impulsivity is the attitude of people who feel the need to do something— anything—immediately.

READING TIME

As you read
Chapter 4:
"Impulsivity:
Do
Something!"
in *The Five
Hazardous
Attitudes*,
reflect on,
and respond
to the text by
answering
the following
questions.

REFLECT AND TAKE ACTION:

Define the Hazardous Attitude of
Impulsivity. How would you describe this
attitude in your own words?

_____

_____

_____

_____

_____

_____

Discuss the tendency of impulsive
individuals to act without thinking first
and the consequences of such behavior.

_____

_____

_____

_____

_____

_____

Explain how the Hazardous Attitude of
Impulsivity can manifest in high-stakes
circumstances, using the example of
pilots and engine failure.

_____

_____

_____

_____

_____

Explore the concept of seeing people as partners rather than speed bumps and how it relates to the Hazardous Attitude of Impulsivity.

_____

_____

_____

_____

_____

_____

_____

Discuss the metaphor of "little foxes that spoil the vine" and its significance in illustrating impulsive behavior in everyday situations.

_____

_____

_____

_____

_____

_____

Explain how impulsive people tend to exhibit impulsive behavior on every level. What is the importance of recognizing small moments of impulsivity?

_____

_____

_____

_____

_____

_____

Explore the impact of stress and external factors on decision-making, particularly for individuals prone to impulsivity. When have you experienced this?

_____

_____

_____

_____

_____

_____

Discuss the suggested mantra for individuals struggling with impulsivity, "If it's gotta be now, it's gotta be no," and how it can serve as a guide for decision-making.

_____

_____

_____

_____

_____

_____

RESIGNATION: WHAT'S THE USE?

Resignation is a Hazardous Attitude that says, "What's the use?"

READING TIME

As you read Chapter 5: "Resignation: What's the Use?" in *The Five Hazardous Attitudes*, reflect on, and respond to the text by answering the following questions.

REFLECT AND TAKE ACTION:

Summarize Captain Frank Wallace's advice to author Ricky Brown about landing an airplane in four words and explain its significance.

_____

_____

_____

_____

_____

_____

_____

_____

Discuss the importance of intentional actions and responsibility in the context of landing an airplane, drawing parallels to life circumstances.

_____

_____

_____

_____

_____

_____

_____

_____

_____

Explain the Hazardous Attitude of Resignation and how it manifests in individuals who are always surprised by their circumstances.

_____

_____

_____

_____

_____

_____

_____

_____

Explore the concept of living with intentionality and how it contrasts with the "what's the use" mindset associated with Resignation.

_____

_____

_____

_____

_____

_____

_____

_____

Discuss the idea that death is not meant to be a crisis of faith but a fact of life and explore how individuals should respond to the departure of loved ones.

_____

_____

_____

_____

_____

_____

_____

_____

_____

Explain the concept that great leaders turn problems into champions. When have you witnessed this?

_____

_____

_____

_____

_____

_____

_____

_____

_____

Explore the impact of putting a person in leadership before their time and the importance of leaders not resigning in the face of challenges.

_____

_____

_____

_____

_____

_____

_____

_____

Discuss the idea of "preaching to the parade" and its relevance to leadership, particularly in handling the loss of relationships within an organization.

_____

_____

_____

_____

_____

_____

_____

_____

_____

Reflect on the concept of saying "hi and bye" as a leader and how accepting the inevitability of people coming and going contributes to effective leadership.

_____

_____

_____

_____

_____

_____

_____

_____

_____

_____

THE TOOLBOX

Words shape worlds. Words shape our behavior patterns and help us envision the outcomes we desire.

READING TIME

As you read
Chapter 6:
"The Toolbox"
in *The Five
Hazardous
Attitudes*,
reflect on,
and respond
to the text by
answering
the following
questions.

REFLECT AND TAKE ACTION:

What are the two primary benefits of
saying something out loud?

_____

_____

_____

_____

_____

_____

_____

_____

_____

_____

How does saying something out loud help
individuals envision the desired outcome,
as illustrated with the example of the
word "orange"?

_____

_____

_____

_____

_____

_____

_____

_____

_____

_____

Explain the significance of the idea that words can shape behavioral patterns and why saying one thing out loud while doing the opposite may indicate a larger problem.

_____

_____

_____

_____

_____

_____

_____

_____

What are the three ways to manage risks associated with Hazardous Attitudes?

_____

_____

_____

_____

_____

_____

_____

_____

Discuss the importance of identifying the Hazardous Attitude before reacting, using personal experiences and outcomes as a guide. Which Hazardous Attitude have you struggled with?

_____

_____

_____

_____

_____

_____

_____

_____

_____

How does measuring the risk associated with a Hazardous Attitude contribute to reconsideration and potential behavior change?

_____

_____

_____

_____

_____

_____

_____

_____

Explain the process of applying the antidote once the risk has been identified and measured and why saying it out loud is emphasized.

_____

_____

_____

_____

_____

_____

_____

_____

Define and discuss the concept of "personal minimums" for pilots and how it can be applied to individuals dealing with Hazardous Attitudes in life.

_____

_____

_____

_____

_____

_____

_____

_____

Provide examples of how personal minimums can be set for macho and impulsive individuals.

_____

_____

_____

_____

_____

_____

_____

_____

_____

Reflect on the idea that personal minimums can save individuals from themselves and how setting them ahead of time helps in knowing when to apply the antidote.

_____

_____

_____

_____

_____

_____

_____

_____

_____

_____

CHAPTER 7

THE APPEAL

That's my hope and prayer for all who read this book, that God would not only change your heart but the hearts of all who come after you to fully live!

READING TIME

As you read
Chapter 7:
"The Appeal"
in *The Five
Hazardous
Attitudes*,
reflect on,
and respond
to the text by
answering
the following
questions.

REFLECT AND TAKE ACTION:

Why is this chapter the "most important chapter in this book"?

_____

_____

_____

_____

_____

_____

_____

_____

_____

_____

_____

_____

_____

_____

_____

_____

_____

_____

_____

_____

_____

_____

The heart is deceitful above all things, and desperately wicked; Who can know it? I, the LORD, search the heart, I test the mind, even to give every man according to his ways according to the fruit of his doings.
—Jeremiah 17:9-10 (NKJV)

Consider the scripture above and answer the following questions:

What stands out to you from this passage of scripture?

_____

_____

_____

_____

_____

How is the heart portrayed in these verses?

_____

_____

_____

_____

_____

How has your heart deceived you in the past?

_____

_____

_____

_____

_____

_____

What is revealed through the verse in the text, Deuteronomy
30:6 (NLT)? How is this verse connected to the theme of heart
change?

_____

_____

_____

_____

Summarize the message regarding salvation and eternal life,
as explained in this chapter. What simple steps are suggested
for someone seeking salvation, and why is saying it out loud
emphasized in this context?

_____

_____

_____

_____

_____

_____

_____

_____

_____

NOTES

www.ingramcontent.com/pod-product-compliance
Lightning Source LLC
Chambersburg PA
CBHW070051100426
42734CB00040B/2985